My Favorite Christmas Story

My Favorite Christmas Story

ROY ROGERS

WITH FRANK S. MEAD

FLEMING H. REVELL COMPANY

To
the boys and girls
everywhere
whose prayers and friendship have
played such an important part
in my life
this little book is humbly dedicated

Library of Congress Catalog Card Number: 60–13095

Printed in the United States of America

CHRISTMAS IS REAL TO ROY

IN THE FOLLOWING pages you will read what Roy Rogers feels about Christmas. . . .

In 1945, one day during the filming of one of his Western musicals, Roy and I were discussing our sentiments about Christmas. He said, "I can't understand anyone not appreciating a gift, no matter what the size. When I was a kid, we didn't have enough money to buy all the things kids get nowadays for Christmas. But I loved my one toy—a brand spanking new, shiny pocket-knife! You know, a kid in the country without a pocketknife is a lost cause! I whittled my own toys all year with that Christmas knife. One Christmas Day it slipped out of my pocket and

I cried so hard and so long that Pop had to go buy me another one next day!"

To this day, Roy's face lights up like a Christmas tree when he receives a gift. What a smile! But the greatest smile I ever saw on his face was the night he received the Gift Supreme—eternal life through putting his faith in the Lord Jesus Christ as his Saviour. This indeed was Christmas in the heart of Roy Rogers, for instead of a pocketknife, he received the shining sword of spiritual truth with which to fashion a new wonderful life! I know—for I was there and witnessed it.

Roy does not like to write, but he is quick to give reason for the hope that is in him. He gave this to our good friend, the esteemed editor of Fleming H. Revell Company, Dr. Frank S. Mead, and we are grateful to him for rounding up Roy's Christmas thoughts.

DALE EVANS ROGERS

☆ **I** ☆

I'm fed up with Christmas

THAT SOUNDS A little stupid, doesn't it, coming from a fellow who goes to church as often as he can and who prays regularly and who thinks the Christ born at Christmas is the greatest gift God ever gave to anybody—including me? Maybe I'd better explain what I mean, so you won't think I'm a turncoat or a crank.

What I mean is that I'm fed up with what a lot of us are *doing* with Christmas. Out here in the West we have a weed we call loco; it grows wild in the range grass, and it drives the cattle loco, or crazy, when they eat it. I think we have all gone a little loco about Christmas—like those crazy cowboys who shoot up the town on payday, in the movies. We've almost shot Christmas to pieces, and that's wrong, in my book.

You can see it in a lot of the stories that are written every Christmas, by good folks who mean well enough and who can write better than I can, but who miss the target by a mile when they sit down to tell us what Christmas is all about, and how we ought to celebrate it. Some of those stories are good—like Dickens' *Christmas Carol*—but too many of them are a waste of time to read. I've just read one of them, about how some fellows spent Christmas Eve in a night club, and how they chipped in to buy a kid a lot of toys. They probably spent ten times more on highballs, that night, than they did on the toys, but they went home to sleep it off (on Christmas Day!), real happy that they'd "kept the Christmas spirit." There was another story about a youngster who grew up to be a famous prize fighter; he got a set of boxing gloves for Christmas, and he spent the best part of the holiest day in the year slugging his pals dizzy and getting slugged dizzy himself.

That's *Christmas?* You can read a whole car-load of stories like that, and you won't find the Bethlehem Baby in one of them.

Maybe I'm getting a little soft in the heart (I

hope so!) and maybe I'm just a sentimental cow-poke, but I don't get it. To me, leaving the Baby out of *any* Christmas story is like leaving the salt out of your food. Any story that does that is as useless as the pony express or the stage-coach.

For me, there's only one Christmas story. It sticks up like Pike's Peak. It has made all sorts of people happy for nearly twenty centuries, and it'll be told twenty centuries from now. Every time I hear it or read it I feel like singing, or going off somewhere to just think about it, and let it run warm through my heart.

It's my favorite Christmas story. A tax-collector named Matthew and a doctor named Luke tell it in the Bible, and it goes like this. . . .

☆ **II** ☆

"Now when Jesus was born in Bethlehem of Judea in the days of Herod the king...."

THAT WAS ABOUT two thousand years ago, and it happened 'way off in a little town in one of the smallest countries in the world. I'll bet there wasn't one in a thousand in the old Roman Empire who could tell you where Judea was, or one in ten thousand who could tell you how to get to Bethlehem. Funny, isn't it, that people all over the world this year will be thinking and talking about Bethlehem and the Baby born there? Or maybe it isn't so funny, at that; God planned it that way. . . .

We'll all be singing about Jesus, but nobody

will be singing about Herod, the "king of Judea." There was a mean polecat, that Herod. He was one of those ornery characters who will do anything to get what he wants. He wanted to be a king, and he really went after it, with his guns out of both holsters. He murdered his favorite wife (he had ten wives, and I guess that was one thing that was the matter with him), her brother and her grandfather, and some of his own children; he bribed anybody low enough to be bribed, among the politicians, and he killed anybody he couldn't buy, to get that throne. It's a good thing he didn't have a six-shooter or a machine gun; there wouldn't have been anybody left. He was mean, and deadly, and so were the Romans who were running the world and Judea, right then. The Roman Emperor probably didn't like the little murderous upstart, but he knew a determined man when he saw one, so he said to this little Hitler, "All right—you can be king of Judea." (Judea was only about fifty-five miles long and fifty-five wide, smaller than the state of Delaware, which looks like a pretty small "kingdom" to me.) ". . . All right, you can be king of Judea. You can rule for us. Just make the people behave, and be a good boy yourself, and

16

do what we tell you to do, or else. . . ." That's
how Herod got his little sawed-off kingdom.
He got to be "king of the Jews," and every Jew
from Dan to Beersheba hated him like we hate
a rattlesnake. (Herod wasn't a Jew, even though
he was born in Palestine; he was an Edomite, and
no Jew ever liked *any* Edomite.) He built a big
beautiful Temple for the Jews in Jerusalem—
and clobbered them with new taxes to pay for
it. They didn't like that. This was the Temple
Jesus saw, in Jerusalem. He didn't think much
of it, either.

That's the way things were, "when Jesus was
born in Bethlehem of Judea in the days of Herod
the king." There was fear and terror and bitter-
ness and blood all over the place. And poverty.
There wasn't enough freedom to put in a ten-
gallon hat; it was all blood and sweat and toil
and tears. And taxes.

God got tired of Herod along about A.D. 4,
and took him out of the way. That's a habit God
has; He seems to let the big bloody tyrants and
trigger-men go just so far, and then—out! He
took Herod, but just before he died the old
rascal put on a real spectacular. He heard that a
new "king" had been born in Bethlehem (five

17

miles from Jerusalem), and he figured that while this "king" might be no king at all, but just something made up in the minds of a lot of superstitious people, he couldn't afford to take any chances. No king likes a rival king. So he ordered his soldiers to go out and kill every baby in Bethlehem. It's hard to believe that even as vicious an hombre as Herod could think up anything like that, but the Bible says he did.

Herod lost out, at that. The Baby was taken out of Bethlehem just in time, and the soldiers never found Him. And a little while later Herod died, and the Baby grew up to be a king with a kingdom and a power that Herod never dreamed of: He became king of the human heart.

This I believe, because He's king in my heart, and because I believe in Christmas.

Old Herod was gone. But there were still taxes.

☆ **III** ☆

"And it came to pass, in those days, that there went out a decree from Caesar Augustus, that all the world should be taxed."

WE PAY TAXES in the United States, and we grumble when we pay, and we say it isn't fair. We should have been around when Caesar Augustus was foreman of the ranch! If you were a Jew in Judea in his time, you paid and paid and paid. First of all, you paid Jewish taxes; you paid for the support of the Temple—which meant paying to keep the priests, who really had it good; every male Jew over twelve years of age kicked in to keep those priests living in luxury, on the fat of the land; he paid a half-shekel poll tax, or "Temple tribute." There was also a tithe on crops, cattle, wheat, figs, olives on the tree and grapes on the vine, barley and honey. Whenever a special day or event came around, there was a tax to help you celebrate it: when a first-born son came along, or a male animal was born, you paid a five-shekel thank offering whether you were thankful or not; if you sinned you paid a tax whether you were sorry about sinning or not; you gave meat "offerings" and "trespass" offerings and there was always a "special drive" for some special purpose being put on by the priests and Temple elders.

When you had paid up your Jewish taxes, Caesar Augustus and his Romans went to work on your pocketbook. They taxed you for the fine "Roman" roads they built across your land; if you crossed a bridge in your travels, you paid a Roman bridge tax; if you went to the theatre, they got you again; if you went into the Temple Herod had built to the Emperor's glory in Samaria, you paid. You couldn't get a drink of water or a mouthful of food without paying off the Romans; you even paid a salt tax, to flavor your food. You paid property tax, village tax, city tax. To help Caesar pay his retired soldiers a pension, there was an additional "purchase" tax. If the Romans improved your town, you got the bill, and you were supposed to be grateful for the improvements.

If you bought or sold anything inside Judea or beyond Judea, you paid a tax; you even paid a tax when you went up to the Temple to pray. You paid, or they took your house and your land; they could draft you into the army or sell you into slavery, if you didn't pay cash on the line. The tax collector could put a false value on your possessions, and you paid; or they could loan you the money for the tax, and charge you 25 per cent interest! If you died, there were "death duties." It was nice, for Caesar Augustus. He got rich, and poor Judea got poorer; how much he took out of there, we'll never know.

Augustus may have wanted to build himself a new palace in Rome, when he decided that "all the world should be taxed." He didn't spare anybody; the whole world was to pay him. And in order to know just how many he could collect from, and how much he could load on each man and woman, he took a census. "And all went to be taxed, every one into his own city." That meant that every man and woman in Palestine had to go and register and sign the tax-roll in the city or town his family came from.

Up in Nazareth lived Joseph and Mary; they packed up, and started down the long road to Bethlehem, the town of Joseph's family. Joseph didn't exactly like the idea of that trip, for Mary was about to have a baby, and Bethlehem is sixty miles from Nazareth, as the crow flies. By way of the long twisting road, it was nearly ninety, and Joseph didn't own a car, and there were no buses or railroads, so they *walked*. Joseph walked, anyway; the artists who have painted pictures of it show Mary riding on a little donkey, and I guess they are right, for no woman about to give birth to a baby could have taken a hike like that. Joseph was a carpenter, with good muscles, but Mary . . . even on a donkey . . . ninety miles!

She was so sick and exhausted by the time they got to Bethlehem that she couldn't have gone another mile. I wonder what she was thinking when they came into that little town after dark; I wonder if she was remembering what her cousin Elizabeth had said to her, some time before: "Blessed art thou among women, and blessed is the fruit of thy womb." How blessed was she now—so tired she could scream, and without a roof over her head or a place to lie down and sleep? What was blessed about all that?

Yet in her heart she knew how blessed she was, for God had chosen her, out of all the women in the world, to give the world this Baby. This wasn't Joseph's baby at all; this was the Son of God waiting to be born in Bethlehem. I think the blessedness came back to her when she thought of that, and while she was a little afraid, as any mother is afraid when any baby is born, she knew everything was going to be all right. God had chosen her, and God would see that everything was all right.

You see, it wasn't any accident that they were in Bethlehem that night; even Caesar Augustus had little to do with it. Long ago, as a child, Mary had read in the old Jewish Scriptures, in the book of Micah the prophet, a promise that this Child of hers was going to be born in Bethlehem: "But thou, Bethlehem . . . though thou be little among the thousands of Judah, yet out of thee shall he come forth unto me that is to be ruler in Israel. . . ." Mary knew this. She

25

knew her Baby was the Promised One, the One promised by the prophets and the Book and God. She knew she was the blessed "handmaid of the Lord," through whom the Son would come.

That's what fascinates me about Christmas. It isn't just a day to pass around presents to everybody, or one day in the year when you're nice to everybody whether you love 'em or loathe 'em; *this is the day God Almighty chose to give us His only begotten Son, through Mary of Nazareth.* How can we miss that?

Most of the folks in Bethlehem missed it, when poor frantic Joseph knocked on the door of a little inn and asked for a room. . . .

☆ IV ☆

"...there was no room for them in the inn."

THERE IS SOMETHING about that knock of Joseph's that hurts. If Joseph and Mary were to ride into your town tonight, you'd have a heart; you'd take them into your home or phone for an ambulance and get them to a hospital. Most of us would do that, because that's the way we are, after two thousand years of Jesus Christ. But people weren't like that in old Bethlehem; they were suspicious of strangers, especially strangers who arrived in the middle of the night. They didn't put "Welcome" on their doormats, in those days. They wouldn't have opened the door for a stranger from Galilee, because the people up there were rough and tough, always fighting the Romans or fighting among themselves. Galileans weren't popular anywhere but in Galilee!

The courtyard of the inn was jammed with donkeys and camels and swearing, weary men. The inn was crowded; there wasn't even standing room. Joseph must have known there wouldn't be any room for him and his Mary, but he knocked, anyway. What else could he do?

Knock, knock, knock. A baby is about to be born. The most important baby ever to be born on this earth. Let us in, let Him in, out of the cold and the night. Knock, knock, knock.

The sleepy innkeeper came rubbing his eyes, and opened the door. He didn't waste any words; he just told them there wasn't any room. They'd have to go somewhere else.

"No room." They are the most heart-rending words in the Bible. No room. Would you have said that? *Don't* you say it, every day? Don't you say it to Christ when He asks you for your heart: "Go away and let me sleep. I've got no time for you, no room in my heart. . . . I don't know you"? We're all innkeepers, with room for everybody and everything but Him. Not many of us really let Him in. I heard once about

an old Scottish minister who used to go around knocking on the doors of his town and asking whoever answered the knock, "Does Jesus Christ live here?" People stared at him and told jokes about him. They thought he was crazy. But was he? Did those jokers wisecrack to cover up a guilty conscience?

But you know, sometimes I feel sorry for that innkeeper, just as I feel sorry for anyone who turns a cold shoulder on Jesus Christ. He just didn't know what was happening, and what he was missing. He just said "no room"—as cold as the ice in Alaska. I think he'd have taken them in, if he'd known. Maybe we've been a little rough on him, criticizing him as we do. To me he was like a fellow wandering in a desert, stumbling along in the night past a spring of cold water he couldn't see and didn't even know was there.

No room. That's what he said. Then—I figure it this way—then his wife came up behind him and took one look at Mary on her donkey, and told them to go out to the stable. The inn was a rambling old building, with a sort of patio in the center, and around this patio they often carved out little caves, out of the soft limestone rock,

for the pack animals of the travelers who stopped at the inn, or for their own sheep and oxen and donkeys, when the weather got real cold. It just could have been that the innkeeper's wife thought of one of those stables—a woman *would* —and that she fixed up a bed of clean straw, and laid Mary gently down on the straw, and covered her, and sat with her a while. A woman would do that, for women think with their hearts, more than men. The innkeeper was all business; his wife could have been a mother. . . .

I wonder how long we'd keep Christmas, if it were up to the men?

☆ V ☆

"And she brought forth her firstborn son, and wrapped him in swaddling clothes, and laid him in a manger...."

So THE BABY was born in the cold, unfriendly night, in a cave cut in the side of a hill, in a bed of straw, in a stable. In Bethlehem, when you ask to see the place where Christ was born, you are taken to a little rock-bound room. There is a big stone church built above it now, with great high beautiful pillars and altars with gold and silver and precious stones, but people who go there now never pay much attention to that. They hurry through the church and take little candles in their hands and go down a flight of narrow twisting stone stairs worn smooth by the feet of saints and sinners and scholars and common folks, into the little rock cave underneath the floor of

35

the church. They stand there hushed, some of them with big tears running down their cheeks, and they look down at the big golden star set in the floor to mark the place where the manger was, where He was born. Princes and paupers come, high and low, good and bad, just to stand for a few minutes where the innkeeper tried to turn Joseph and Mary and the Baby away. They come into the place through a door that's only four feet high, so low that they have to bow to get through it. No matter who or what they are, they bow as they approach the manger.

You stand there, and all the world stands still around you, and you hear nothing and see nothing but the Baby in the feeding-box where the oxen came to eat, and if you've got a heart, it breaks.

That's Christmas, to me: standing at the manger. . . .

It was a stable, yes, a mean place for a baby to be born, a mean place even for animals. It wasn't nearly as fine a stable as Trigger has. It wasn't the light, shining place the artists have painted; it was a dark, damp hole in the ground. Here He was born. You don't like it? You think the Son of God should have been born in a palace, or at least in a place where there wasn't any dirt or darkness? But that wouldn't have been right, because God was sending His Son into a world that was a filthy stable, a world dark with pain and hatred and dirty with sin. It was right for Him to be born here, for He had come to make men clean and to bring a light into the world that would drive away the darkness in men's minds. I'm no theologian, and I haven't had an education in theology, and I know this explanation of why He came may not please all the theologians, but that's the way it looks to me. I can't put it in fancy language, but I can say that He brought light and peace and something new and clean and fine into my life, and that's all the theology I need. . . .

Some of the highbrows in Jerusalem got mad at Him, once, because He sat down with a lot of lowbrow sinners and outcasts that the "best people" just didn't associate with. They criticized Him for that; He turned on them and told them He had come to help people like this, and not "the best people," who were so proud and self-righteous they thought they didn't need any help. Some of His best friends were sinners. He came to get them out of the stable. . . .

37

☆ VI ☆

IV

"And there were in the same country shepherds abiding in the field, keeping watch over their flock by night."

AFTER MARY AND JOSEPH, the animals in the stable were the first to see Him, in His swaddling clothes. Maybe there was a young calf there, and maybe that reminded the Jews in the inn that His people had once worshiped a golden calf. Or an ox: there were some people who worshiped oxen. Or a sheep, marked for sacrifice that week in the Temple at Jerusalem. But now that the Baby had come the sacrifice of animals was on the way out; men would not worship or sacrifice beasts any more; they would worship

41

the Christ who lay in the straw. The breath and the warm bodies of the animals warmed Him, in the little room. If they could have talked, what would they have said to Him? What would the lambs have said to the Lamb of God who would be sacrificed on a cross?

The animals—then the shepherds from the hills. The shepherds were the first men to come. The people in the courtyard may have looked in at Him, and smiled, and gone away never knowing what they had seen, but the shepherds *came*, and they came because they knew, and they came to worship. Out on their hillsides, watching their sheep, they had heard a great strange music. If *you* will go out this Christmas Eve and stand still and just look up at the stars, and listen, you can hear it, too—the music that comes from behind the stars, from another world. You can hear it, if you'll listen.

The shepherds heard the angels sing: "Glory to God in the highest, and on earth peace, good will. . . ." Peace? For the shepherds, who got kicked around by everybody? Good will? Who had anything good to say about a shepherd? You were really out of luck, if you had to watch sheep for a living; that was about as far down

as you could go. But my Bible says the shepherds
heard it first, and that they came first to worship
the little King who would make them the equals
of anyone in the world. They had waited a
long, long time for this night—ever since Abra-
ham was a shepherd in Ur, ever since David was
a shepherd in Bethlehem, they had waited. Now
they came running into Bethlehem, *believing
what the angels had told them*. They came first
because they were the first to understand that
this was the Good Shepherd. . . .

They were poor, so they couldn't have brought
any Christmas presents—oh, maybe a little milk,
or wool, or a baby lamb. But their gifts weren't
important. *They brought themselves*. It was all
the Baby would have wanted from them. Did
you ever stop to think, at Christmas, that the
only gift He wants from you is you?

Christmas is giving time—time for giving ourselves.

We don't think enough about those shepherds.
We talk about how they came to Bethlehem;
how about looking at how they *left* Bethlehem?
They left it "glorifying and praising God"—
and man, that's important. I'll bet they sang all
the way home. Anyone who meets Jesus Christ

goes away singing. It's a little like going to church; you can't go there without feeling better.

Something happened to the shepherds. They didn't go home and sit around the rest of their lives dreaming about what happened that night. They told everybody about it, and "all who heard about it wondered." It figures. They had to tell everybody. I never knew a happy man who was a quiet man, who could keep his mouth shut about whatever it is that is making him happy.

Christmas is telling time—wondering time. Wonder enough about it, and you'll know, and you'll tell about it. . . .

My mother and father told me about these shepherds when I was a kid, and I never could get them out of my mind. These shepherds never went to school, never wrote any books, probably couldn't read or write. But they were the first Christian preachers; and I've got a sneaking suspicion that the folks who listened to them didn't care very much that they couldn't read or write, or that they were shepherds. The people knew they were listening to eyewitnesses. Some of the best preachers I've ever listened to never saw the inside of a college, but they had something in-

44

MY FAVORITE CHRISTMAS STORY

side them that was good, and they threw it right at me, and it stuck. I think the shepherds were like that.

Once I heard about an old hermit down in Egypt, who lived four hundred years after the shepherds were dead and gone. This old fellow lived in a cave, where he worshiped God day and night, at a time when the scholars and the bishops and the theologians in the city were getting themselves—and everybody else—in one grand and glorious snarl, arguing about Jesus Christ. Some of them said Jesus was just a man, and some said He was just God and not man at all, and some said He was the Son of God, and some said He was both God and Son of God, and. . . . It all got pretty confusing. After a while they brought the old man into town. They asked him if he thought Jesus was the Christ, the Messiah. They figured he'd know, if anybody did; he'd lived so close to God for so long that the people were calling him a saint—Saint Anthony. He looked at them in amazement, and he said, "I have *seen* Him!" He had seen the Christ, and he knew. So had the shepherds.

Christmas is seeing time. If you can't see Him then, you may never see Him.

a strange star they had never seen before, as a ship is steered by the stars. They came down the same old road the Queen of Sheba had come down, a thousand years before, to visit Solomon, the wisest man in the world, to ask him questions, and give him gifts of gold, and rare perfumes. . . .

They turned up in Jerusalem, first; I'd guess they got off the road, or that one of King Herod's patrols picked them up and brought them in as suspicious characters, for questioning. And I'd guess old Herod was scared half out of his wits, too, when he saw them. He'd heard the gossip about the baby "King" born in Bethlehem, and he didn't like it; if this Bethlehem Baby was all people said He was, there could be trouble. All these people who hated the sight of Herod could start a revolution around the King in Bethlehem. There must be *something* to it; these wise men hadn't come all the way from Persia for nothing.

Herod was clever, though; give him credit for that. "All right," he said to the wise men. "All right. Go to Bethlehem and see what's going on down there, and then come back and report to me, so I can go and worship Him." There was murder in his eye when he said it.

"...behold, there came wise men from the east...."

THE WISE MEN came to Bethlehem, too. Do you suppose the shepherds met them on the road? If they did, what did they have to say to each other?

These wise men came from the East—that could mean from Persia—and if you know what I mean, they were big league, or something special. The kings, in the East, were pretty powerful; the kings told the people what to do—but the wise men told the kings. They knew just about everything there was to know about what was going on in the world—*and* in heaven! They had all the answers; they read secrets in the stars and they came all the way from Persia guided by

So they went out, and looked up in the sky for the star, and—"When they saw the star, they rejoiced with exceeding great joy." They found Him there in the stable, and they got down on their knees and worshiped Him.

Then they unpacked their bags and laid out on the floor of the stable the gifts they had brought all the way from Persia. They were gifts you'd never buy in a five-and-ten-cent store, for these men were rich as well as wise. They brought gold—and laid it at the feet of Jesus Christ, at the feet of One who was to be poor until He died, who was born in a borrowed manger, who was to eat borrowed food at the tables of His friends, who was to die on a borrowed cross and be buried in a borrowed garden, who was to say to a man with much gold, "Sell all thou hast, and give it to the poor." At His feet the wisest men in the world threw their gold, as if they were saying, "You're right. Your way is best." It was something new. Up to then, you measured a man by his gold, by the size of his strongbox. You were somebody if you were rich, and nobody if you weren't. This Baby—did the wise men know it?—gave us a new yard-stick for measuring the worth of a man; you were somebody, He said, if you were a servant. Gold had a brand-new use: it was good only to help others, to help the poor. . . .

They gave Him frankincense. Let's call it incense, for that's what it was—a sweet-smelling offering that was burned in the incense pots of the Temple. The Jews burned incense in their great rituals in the Temple at Jerusalem, and the wise men, all their lives, had seen it burned in their pagan temples far from Jerusalem—burned as wistful, wishful offerings of faith and hope before the unmoving idols of the pagan world. It rose up into the faces of these clay-faced gods. Of course the gods couldn't help, but the worshipers were sincere enough; their burning frankincense had to do with the things of the spirit, and that was good.

But it was better, now, to bring incense to a *living* God. And when they dropped that incense at the feet of this living God in Christ, they were offering *their* lives as incense, too. They were adding living to ritual, if you know what I mean. God demands that of all of us: He wants our lives burned out for Him. If we can't give Him our lives, we might as well save our incense.

It's something like this. You know my horse

☆ VII ☆

Trigger? He's pretty smart. We do quite a few tricks together, at rodeos and county fairs. Trigger can dance, step around to music, and he can take a bow like a real ham actor. It looks so easy—but it takes days and weeks of practice, on the ranch in San Fernando Valley, to get those tricks smooth and right. We go through a sort of ritual at the rodeos, and the folks like it. (Maybe ritual isn't the right word, but you'll know what I mean.) But a lot of the folks will never know how much practice it takes, before we get out there. It takes a lot of practice to make a Christian—*a lot of good living*.

So here in the stable the wise men threw their precious frankincense at the feet of Jesus, as if they were saying, "From now on we'll burn out our lives in Your service."

And myrrh. They gave Him myrrh. Myrrh was even more important than frankincense; it was an expensive perfume (the Chanel No. 5 of the court ladies), and the priests used to put it in the oil they used to anoint other priests, and kings, and the sick. It was a gum from the myrrh tree that relieved pain; the Roman soldiers gave Jesus wine mixed with myrrh while He hung on the cross. And Nicodemus brought myrrh for the embalming of His body, when He died. But they couldn't have been thinking of all that when they brought it to the Baby in the stable; it was just a rare, costly gift fit for a king. I wonder, though, if they might have been thinking a little about healing—about the healing of broken hearts and lives, and the "healing of nations" that had come to earth with this Baby. . . . Wealth, worship, healing . . . it could be.

Three wise men from the East, bearing gifts. We don't even know their names; they are supposed to be named Caspar, Melchior and Balthazar, but the Bible doesn't name them. It doesn't even say there were three of them. There might have been more, or less. It doesn't make much difference. It wasn't how many of them there were, but what they did, that counts.

They brought gifts—expensive gifts. Is that where we got the idea that we all have to break the bank to buy expensive gifts at Christmas— that we have to go broke to prove we've got the Christmas spirit? I get sick all over just standing in the stores at Christmas time, watching people throw their money around like loco cowboys on payday. They put on mob scenes that would go good in the movies, fighting each other to buy a lot of overpriced junk (you can get it at half price the day after Christmas!) that most of their friends don't want, with money they haven't got, or shouldn't be spending if they have got it —for what? We beat our brains out trying to think of something to give someone who doesn't need anything. I saw a sign in one department store that told me this was a department filled with expensive odds and ends "for the man who has everything." Well, if he has everything, why give him more? Maybe he'd appreciate it more if you'd come around to see him when he's sick, or give him a hand when he's in trouble.

There used to be a society called SPUG— "The Society for the Prevention of Useless Giving." What ever became of that? It was a good idea.

Why do we do it? Why do we commercialize Christmas like this? Do we have to throw money away to prove we aren't "cheap" about Christmas? To me, we cheapen ourselves when we celebrate the King's birthday with a one-day spending spree, and then forget Him all the rest of the year. If that's the Christmas spirit, I don't want it.

Sure, the wise men brought gifts—*for Jesus*

Christ. They gave *Him* their gold; they gave *Him* their frankincense and myrrh. And they took something away. They didn't just drop their presents under the tree and say "Merry Christmas" and then go out and forget it until next Christmas. *They turned their backs on an old, wrong way of life and walked off with God.* They brought their gifts to God, not to any man; they saw God in the manger, and the sight of Him made them different men.

Christmas shouldn't be spending time; it should be changing time.

☆ VIII ☆

"And ... they departed into their own country another way."

THAT'S WHAT MATTHEW says they did, after they had left their gifts: they went back by a different road. Oh, yes, they were "warned of God in a dream that they should not return to Herod," but to me that's only half of it. I think they'd have gone home that way even without that dream; old Herod would have killed them, and they knew it. The important thing is that the road back was *different*. Everything was changed. Every hut and stable gleamed with light. Every woman was a Mary. Every crude, cursing man was loved of God, with a new Friend back in Bethlehem. Every shepherd seemed a new kind of man, a man with ears tuned to hear the angels sing. It was a different road, a different world. God was in it now, as He had never been in it before.

The shepherds first, then the wise men: first the lowly, then the great. I've always been glad those wise men came, even if they did get there a little late. They were running true to form, coming late; the fellows with lots of brains *always* come late. They have to fight their way through a lot of brain-problems that never bother the rest of us—but they come. The really intelligent man comes to the manger, and gets down on his knees. The greatest astronomer always finds His star, and stands silent as he looks at it.

I'm told there's an island in the Caribbean Sea where a lot of Yale and Harvard professors spend their vacations every summer, and that on that island there is a blacksmith who teaches a Sunday school class for grown-ups. The professors come every Sunday to hear him; it's the best part of their vacations. They just sit and listen to him. He's got something they never found in books—and they want it.

The *really* wise always come. . . .

☆ **IX** ☆

"Let us go now even unto Bethlehem. . . ."

I s'pose I'll be in California, this Christmas. I'd like to be in Bethlehem. Wouldn't you? Well—let's go! Let's have a Bethlehem Christmas this year, wherever we are. We don't have to travel. All we have to do is to turn our hearts into a manger and let Him be born there. Can I ask you something here, without making you mad? *If He isn't born in your heart, what difference does it make to you whether He was born in Bethlehem or not?*

I heard another good story the other day. Seems there was a little girl looking at the Nativity scene they'd set up in her church, for Christmas. She looked a long time at the face of the little wax doll they'd laid there in the straw, to represent the Baby, and then she said, "He's a lot more alive than that." Smart girl! She said it for me. She saw what I wish all of us could see in this great Christmas story: that Bethlehem is *now*, that He is here just as much as He was in the stable of the inn that night, waiting for us to come, to give ourselves. . . .

Let's all go even unto Bethlehem.

May the good Lord of Christmas take a liking to you, and a Bethlehem Christmas to you all.